AUTUMN'S DIARY OF DREAMS

BY

ALEXANDRA ANDRAS

Copyright © 2022, Alexandra Andras

All rights reserved. The use of any part of this publication, reproduced, transmitted in any form or by any means, electronic, mechanical, photocopying, recording or otherwise stored in a retrieval system, without the prior consent of the publisher is an infringement of the copyright law.

First edition.
Published by Book Writing Founders.
Highland Park, IL 60035

Many of my clients went out of their way to recount them experiences for this project, and their generosity has helped make this a better book. While there is tremendous value in these experiences for you, my reader, there is also tremendous value for my clients in moving on from them. With this in mind and to maintain anonymity, I've changed names and specific details for the client quotes and experiences. Any resemblance to persons living or deceased is entirely coincidental and unintentional.

The contents herein are not intended to treat, diagnose, or in any part offer professional counselling for any physical or psychological disorders. The author and publisher do not dispense medical advice or prescribe the use of any technique as a form of treatment for physical, emotional, or medical problems without the advice of a physician, in any instance. The author and publisher are not responsible or liable for any loss or damage, emotional, physical, or otherwise, allegedly arising from any information or suggestions contained within this book.

DEDICATION

This book is dedicated to my loving parents, brother and rest of my family who have faith in me and always support me no matter what. Also, it is dedicated to my perfect teachers, from Southfields Primary School, who coax a smile onto my face every day.

ACKNOWLEDGEMENT

A big thank you to the people who have worked with me to publish this book.

Another thank you to all my loving, caring family who motivated me and have had supported me.

I then mustn't forget my caring teachers from Southfields Primary School.

ABOUT THE AUTHOR

My name is Alexandra Andras. I am an ordinary 10 years old girl who lives in the city Peterborough in England. I was born in December 2012, as a Christmas gift for my parents. Although I am British, my family's roots reach all the way to Eastern Europe. My parents moved to Peterborough from a small town in Slovakia called Kežmarok.

I live with my Mum, Dad, little brother and two rabbits. I go to Southfields Primary School. I adore school and education generally, whereas, my favourite subject is either Literacy or Handwriting.

I enjoy reading and writing which had inspired me to write stories.

When I am not at school, I like dancing and drawing. One of my greatest achievements is writing this book! My favourite hobby to do anywhere is to read, read, read and read.

My favourite author that I like to read is Sophie Anderson. Not only do I like reading but, I also enjoy writing. When I am older, I would like to become an author.

In the future, I would like to write drama or mystery.

PROLOGUE

I am Autumn Mayster.

I am 12 years old. I lived in Milton Keynes with my Mum, Dad, little brother and, dog, Ascher. I lived in a small cottage in a rather empty village.

Our village was empty because it was in the infinite fields that nobody ever went to. Me and my family move quite often due to school and work.

I have lived in many different houses, cottages, and flats. Every evening, we all sit by the fireplace and stare at the night sky, in search for comets and shooting stars. If we are lucky enough to find a gleaming celestial body, we would crouch and gather by the fire, each making a wish.

My dog, Ascher, is a Bernese Mountain Dog and he loves to play. We raised him as a pup because he was an orphan and lost his parents in an avalanche.

It is hard to move houses often with a dog because once we move in, Ascher would sniff the entire house before we go inside. It is his way of letting us know if it is 'safe'.

Living with family is great, especially if you have a loving one. I cannot help but say, I have been the luckiest in this department

CONTENTS

Chapter 1: A New Boring Day! 1
Chapter 2: The Exam 3
Chapter 3: Enemies & Friends 7
Chapter 4: The Unexpected News. 9
Chapter 5: The Wish 14
Chapter 6: Farewells And Greetings 17
Chapter 7: A Different Discovery 20
Chapter 8: The Conversation: 25
Chapter 9: Jinx 30
Chapter 10: The Plan 33
Chapter 11: Bravery And Fear 38
Chapter 12: The Memory 41
Chapter 13: Miss Clémentine 45
Chapter 14: A Great Experience 47
Chapter 15: The Forgiveness 49

Epilogue 52

Chapter 1
A NEW BORING DAY!

ONE MORNING at 7:00a.m, I was still fast asleep in my bed, dreaming of many things. Books really. Suddenly, something disturbed my fantasy world. Or should I say, someone?

It was Mum. "Autumn Mayster, up now, you have school today."

School. I hate it. My French teacher, Mrs Jeanues, was the worst! She would yell at you for just mispronouncing a word. I stumbled out of bed and slumped all the way downstairs.

Breakfast was already on the table. A bowl of my favourite Fruit Loops. As I spooned my cereal into my mouth, Mum asked me, "Have you studied for your Maths exam today?"

"Yes!" I mumbled chomping Loops in my mouth with pride.

As I packed my bag asking myself, "What is 2,381 x 107?," I sighed exhaustedly and heaved my bag onto my back.

I stepped into the gloomy clouds.

Then my bus was out. "Have fun Auts!" bellowed Mum whilst waving frantically.

As I sat myself in the bus, a little four-year-old started asking me questions and telling me

unnecessary things. "Who are you? What are you doing on that phone? Where are you going?"

Then his mother came along. "Mason! I am so sorry!" she apologized with sorry eyes.

"It's alright!" I answered peacefully.

I couldn't think of anything else to do but message my friend. It took us twenty minutes to reach school.

It's as dull as dishwater, as dreary as dusk, there's so many ways to describe it. In bad ways, obviously.

I walked to the door in slow- motion hoping school would be dismissed very early. I entwined my index and middle finger onto each other and leaned into the dim hall. I then went on the search for my locker. I found it. No.4. There were not many students in this school. Clearly. I grabbed my stationary. I then slowly walked into class. The first class was French. Yay. I thought to myself,

"I bet Mrs Jeanues is going to scream so much that she won't even be able to speak for the rest of the day."

I gave a long, bored moan. I flopped towards class. I took a deep breath, exhaled and tiptoed into the classroom. Uh Oh! I decided before class, it wouldn't matter if I splashed my face with some very, very, very, very, very cold water to wake the aliveness out of me. It was time. I tried to stall myself, but that didn't work. I fiddled with my hair to distract myself, but no matter what I did, I would go in. It was taking too long. I would rather have gotten detention. I wasn't very excited....

Chapter 2
THE EXAM

~~~

MRS JEANUES was waiting with a stern look on her face and was tapping her foot.

The half-moon spectacles reflected of the lights and her dry lips pouted.

"Bonjour a' toute la classe," she said in a jolly tone showing her squared teeth.

"Bonjour." the class mumbled with boredom.

In her French accent she inquired, "Now, does anybody know what you are supposedly doing today?"

Benjamin Green - one of my class mates, raised his hand and murmured, "Mathematics exam, Miss?"

"Oui. But unfortunately for those who enjoy mathématiques, instead of that you have Examen de Français!!" she exclaimed joyfully.

The entire class said either "Come on!" or "Seriously!"

Mrs Jeanues danced about and started singing in French. Her dirty-blonde bob bounced and flew across her slightly wrinkled face.

I buried my head in my hands, sighed and thought, can this day get any worse?!

The test was okay. The first question said, "E'crivez votre nom dans la case ci-dessous."

That meant, "Write your name in the box below." I wrote, Mayster d'automne.

The next question was, "Si vous connaissez E=____, alors vous pourrez connaître A2+B2=____."

I thought it said, A2+B2= C2. It turns out, it said, "If $E= Mc^2$, then you shall know A2+B2= C2."

Luckily, I got a B-. Maybe it wasn't worth acting so stressed and disappointed. At lunch, I got my tray and sat by my best friend, Julia Saunders.

"How was French class?" she questioned.

"It wasn't that bad." I answered, "We had a French exam instead of a Mathematics."

"Oh." she tilted her head in confusion.

Julia was my best ever friend. On my first day of school - which I joined in the middle of Year 7, we instantly became companions. We became friends by the fact that we met in the hall. She showed me where my locker was and helped me find the class I was looking for. We were friends ever since.

Once we finished our lunch, the bell rang. We walked to our lockers and put our books inside. As we slammed our doors, the bell rang again. Everyone scurried along and looked a bit baffled.

Autumn's Diary of Dreams

The school speaker whistled. "Year 7, Class 3, your next class is the gym. Hurry up!"

That was Mr Lurkten, the school coach. He wore a red jacket and a whistle. He had a large, round belly and his joggers were old and stretched out. He had a small, chubby face that made his squishy cheeks droop.

I hoped that P.E was going to be better than the recent class that I didn't dare say. I groaned once more and went towards the gymnasium.

E'crivez votre nom
dans la case
ci-dessous
Mrs Jeanues
French Teacher

Chapter 3
ENEMIES & FRIENDS

WHEN WE ARRIVED at the gym, Mr Lurkten told us to do hundred push-ups as a warm up! The jock, Bradley Malton, made it look as if it was two plus two. Then Becky Dayes showed up. She is the 'super popular' girl and every boy would follow her when they see her.

Every school has their enemy. Becky was mine. She would always pass me and say, "What's the matter weirdo!? Is it your poor sense of style?!" or even, "you really think that's a cute outfit?!" She is your classic popular girl.

Lucky for me, she got told off for being late. The main lesson was just as hard as the warm up. We did fifteen laps around the field which was as big as an entire skate park.

After a while, everyone in the field was either guzzling water or panting in a stupidly, silly way.

At 14:00, the bell suddenly rang. We got changed into our original clothes and came to our lockers.

Bradley was coming out of the gym and Becky passed him.

"Hey Brad!", she cried in a flirty way.

I obviously saw, so I scoffed and slammed the locker door with fury.

I went up to Julia and said, "Do you see how Becky always acts whimsy around Bradley?"

She flicked her chocolate coloured hair and looked at me with her emerald-green eyes and said,

"No, I haven't noticed!" she says in Becky's tone of voice. "I really wish she wouldn't be so popular that everybody likes her."

"Mmmhmm.." I drawled slowly.

The bell rang again. I felt so exhausted that I took slow dramatic steps and trudged all the way to the next class.

The last class of the day was Chemistry and it was one of my favourites. As I was exceedingly

tired, I gave my best to seem eager but my face kept drooping continuously. At class, the teacher, Mr Pattricks, was showing us how to mix chemicals safely. "Now, add the Hydrogen Peroxide to the Dry Ice and see if anything happens." he said while holding up two differently coloured beakers.

I added a dry ice cube to the hydrogen and a smoky, steam sort of 'fire' was created.

The entire class went, "Woah!" as they observed the steam flames. I scrutinised the way it wafted and waved in the warm air and how it gently extinguished.

Chapter 4

THE UNEXPECTED NEWS.

I FINALLY was able to go home. I waited for the bus to arrive so I could get home and rest

As I stepped through the chestnut doorway, I saw Mum and Dad sitting on the dining table and discussing something. This something seemed urgent as they both had a serious look on their faces.

"Kids! We have got something to tell you!" sighed Dad flicking his brown hair.

We both came up to the table. "We are going to have to move again," huffed Mum. Her hazelnut eyes narrowed in annoyance.

I was terribly disappointed. Only once have I made a friend and yet again, our friendship was going to be destroyed. I then stomped upstairs into my room and screamed, "I hate that we always have to move and always move school!"

I kicked my table so hard that I made my foot numb. "The whole idea is stupid!" I yelled.

I knelt on my bed and cried. I bawled so hard, that I fell into a deep sleep.

The next morning was a Saturday and I woke up to see a heap of suitcases. My cheeks were still hot with anger and I boomed downstairs. "Good morning Auts!" hooted Jacob, while spooning a bowl of porridge into his mouth. I didn't say anything. I just sat opposite him and put all the moving stuff to the back of my mind.

"Would you like some Loops?" inquired Mum with her soft, kind tone of voice

I nodded and thought about Julia. "What if she replaces me with a new friend?!'

I felt a few bitter tears rub my cheeks, so I sat with my head in my hands and sighed.

Mum sat next to me and said, "What's the matter, my rose?"

Mum had called me that when I was little since it was my favourite flower.

"You know what!" I sobbed with my voice cracking.

Mum pulled me into a hug and most of the rage in my belly had settled down.

I wiped my tears with my sleeve and sniffed. Mum had lay down a bowl of my cereal.

I looked at the bowl and asked, "Where's Dad?"

Mum fell silent and I knew why.

"Oh," I whispered.

"Why do we even have to move?" mumbled Jacob.

"Well, even though both of you have school, me and Dad don't have a job," she said gently.

"As always!" I commented.

Dad came back from the Estate Agency. He took his hat and cloak off and huffed.

He sat in a chair and Mum joined him.

"Any news?" I asked wincing and crossing my fingers.

Jacob looked at Dad hopefully and was murmuring lots of incoherent things.

"Well, we have a new Estate!" he boomed.

I palm-faced myself because Jacob was doing a silly little dance.

"Where is it located?" questioned Mum.

"It is in Manchester!" cried Dad.

Jacob was so happy and bellowed. "Can we go to that Football Stadium!?"

"Yes, yes we can see everything in the city!" giggled Mum.

I distracted myself with my cereal and spoon. I eventually said, "I'm not hungry anymore!" and I trudged upstairs again. I took a suitcase from the pile and started packing my things. I packed all of my precious books, devices, and other parts. I looked through every shelf and drawer until my gaze fell on a picture.

A picture of me when I was a baby and my parents holding me. I felt a smile grow on my face. I put the picture into my pocket and continued packing. I got through quite a few objects such as more books, for example, fantasy from when I was younger and books up to date, glass objects and more devices.

Once I had finished packing my bits and bots, I called Dad over to take my table, bed, closet and shelfs apart.

The only thing I was happy about was that I probably would never see Becky again! But the bad side is that I wouldn't see Julia ever again. I just hoped and wished that I would see Julia again in the future.

Wish! I had the perfect idea.

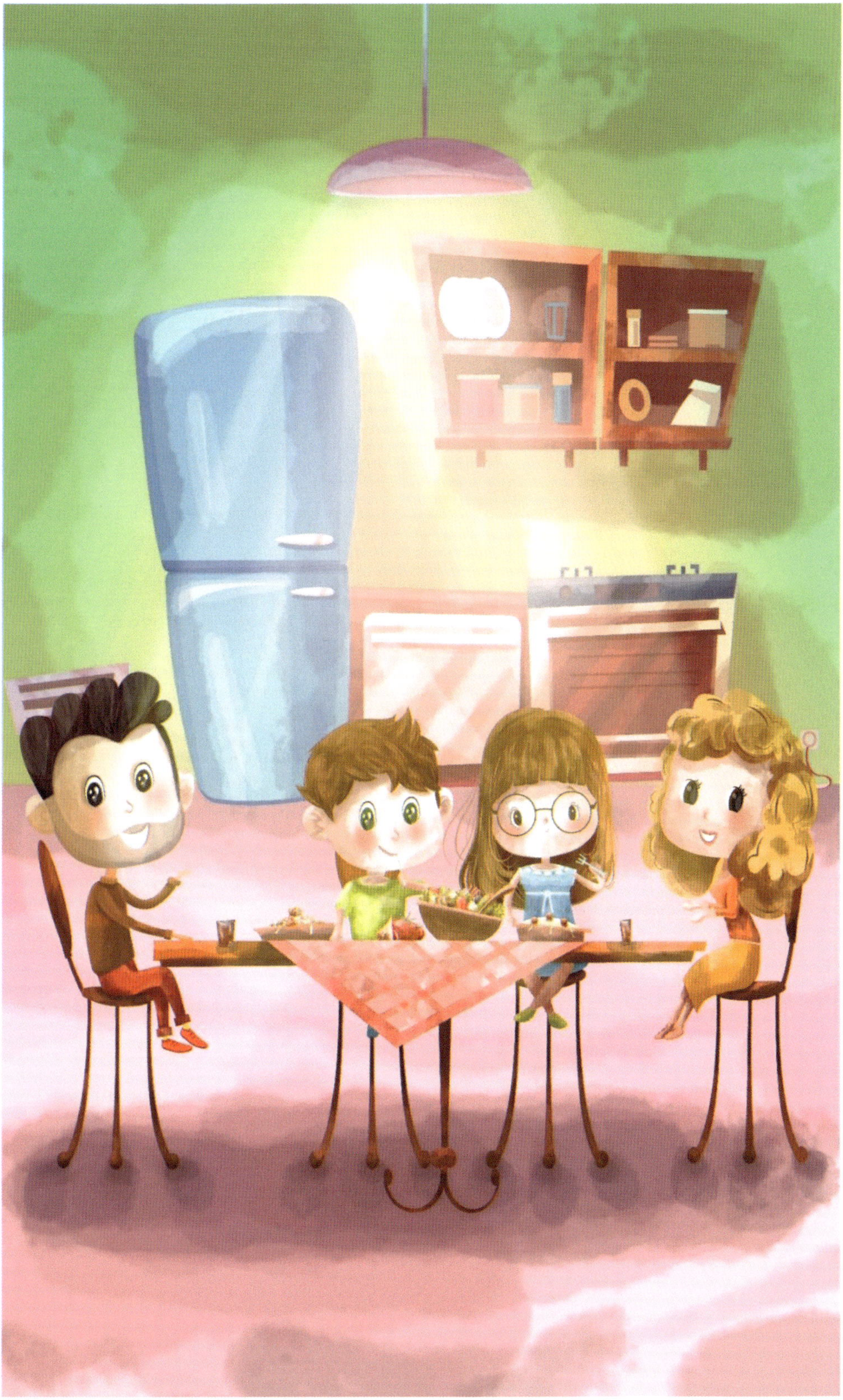

Chapter 5

THE WISH

WHEN IT WAS time to search for comets, I had my wish ready. I held my fingers crossed so that a star would appear. I held my breath and hoped until… WHOOSH! A comet flashed past us. "MUM! DAD! A COMET!" I shrieked.

We all gathered around the fire and got our wishes ready. I started first, "I wish I would see Julia someday again!"

Then Mum wished, "I wish we will fit in Manchester!"

"I wish I will have a happy, healthy family for the rest of my living life!" whispered Dad.

"I wish that we could go to the Football Stadium!" bounced Jacob.

Then Ascher started barking, "Woof, woof, woof, woof, woof."

I imagined what he was trying to say. In the evening, I laid myself on a mattress and sighed. I shut my eyes tight and dreamt of the new house. I tossed and turned and woke up with a gasp. It was a dream.

Autumn's Diary of Dreams

I had this dream for years now and it's getting a bit old for me now. I dreamt that a large clump of dark, black mist had kidnapped my family, even Ascher! I lay my body once again and creaked my eyelids closed, but no matter what I did, I couldn't fall asleep! I sighed and read one of my books. Moby Dick by Herman Melville. I read a few chapters and fell back into a deep slumber.

Suddenly, a ringing sound woke me up. RING! RING! The sound was as shrill as a megaphone feedback that made me feel a bit blank.

"Everybody up!" bellowed a deep booming voice. It was Dad. "Why did you wake us up?" Jacob yawned like an actor. "Well, we have to move at 8:00, so we have to get changed, eat breakfast, brush our teeth, and finish packing our things!" he howled.

"Of course, we have to!" I mumbled and stretched my arms.

I got dressed into my amber coloured, woollen dress, brushed my ginger hair, and put on my beige slippers and raced downstairs. I was down first, so I made everyone breakfast. I made poached egg on bread with fresh chives, ham, and cheese. I would normally eat this because I am Slovakian and we eat this sort of food. I laid the other plates on the table and sat chewing my ham and munching the egg.

As I carefully swallowed my bread, Mum, Dad and Jacob came down. I gulped and gulped. "I made breakfast!" I mentioned with pride. I grinned cheekily and put my plate in the sink and washed it.

"Dad, can we watch the big match on Saturday?" pleaded Jacob.

"Yes, we can watch it but it depends on how much the tickets cost," chuckled Dad but with a smirk on the corner of his mouth.

Jacob danced around the table in his football kit in a foolish way.

"Mum, Dad, I'm going outside to collect some hazelnuts!" I announced.

I grabbed my satchel and stepped outside the pale, dirty white cottage. I smiled softly and ran into the pine forest.

As I strolled on the search for nuts, I spotted a little starling. I ran over to see what was the matter. It turns out the little bird had fell out of its nest. I scooped the poor thing up and wrapped it into my scarf. I looked all over and finally saw a small nest in the trees. I climbed up and placed the little one in the nest with its mother and siblings.

I grinned and said my farewells to the baby and went back to collecting. I had found many different sized hazelnuts, large and small.

I then lead myself back home again.

Chapter 6

FAREWELLS AND GREETINGS

I GOT HOME by 8:00, grabbed all of my cases and loaded them into the van. Once that was done, I adjusted myself in my seat and fastened my seatbelt.

After a minute, Mum, Dad and Jacob came along and also did the same thing as me. Jacob jumped about in his seat constantly as he excitedly inquired, "Are we there yet?"

By the time we arrived, Jacob was finally calmer. However, he whizzed outside hopping as if he needed the bathroom.

Ascher leaped out and barked. "Oh, yes, of course. You can check the area!" Mum said with a giggle. He sniffed and scanned the house and barked. Ruff! Ruff!

I thought he didn't let us, but hopes had fallen.

Mum told us to close our eyes as we went into our rooms. It was a marvel! All the walls had already been painted and all the furniture was there. It was just like at home. Well, it's now our old home.

I gasped and held back my tears as many memories and flashbacks raced through my mind. I laughed and jumped onto my own old bed and mattress. "Well, what do you think?" smiled Dad. I smiled back and said, "It's perfect!"

At 12:00, we had some lunch. Mum went to the shop and had brought some ingredients. I helped her make Jacob's favourite soup, Zeleninova Polievka, which means Vegetable Soup.

As Mum stirred and I peeled the vegetables, Jacob started bouncing a ball eagerly. "I'm going outside to kick about!" He wailed as if he were a ghost. Once the soup was finished, I told Mum that I was going to get Jacob back in.

She nodded her head gently, as I dashed outside and went after him. We both sprinted back for lunch at the very same time.

I laid out some spoons, napkins, and cups. While I was pouring water into the cups, Dad came along and sat on the table. "Do you have any news?" inquired Mum.

"I...," declared Dad, while slapping his knees like a drum, "Have a job!"

Mum cried out in joy, "What are you working as?"

"An.....," resumed Dad, "author!"

I cheered with fulfilment. My own father, an author!

In the late afternoon, I lit the fireplace, opened the curtains and sighed. "Mum, Dad, Jacob, let's look for the stars."

We knelt by the windowsill and foraged for comets. 'WHOO!' A comet flew by. Everybody gathered around the fire and prepared their wish. "I wish we can have enough money to see the Big Match next week!" spoke Jacob and bobbed up and down his knees. "I wish we will have a great life here," desired Mum.

"I wish my job will work out and we will have enough money to buy things," mumbled Dad sleepily.

I went last, "I wish school tomorrow will work out and I will make a friend."

I got changed into my peach-coloured sleep wear and read some Moby Dick. At 20:36, my eyelids felt heavy, my hands were too weak to hold up a book and I dropped to sleep.

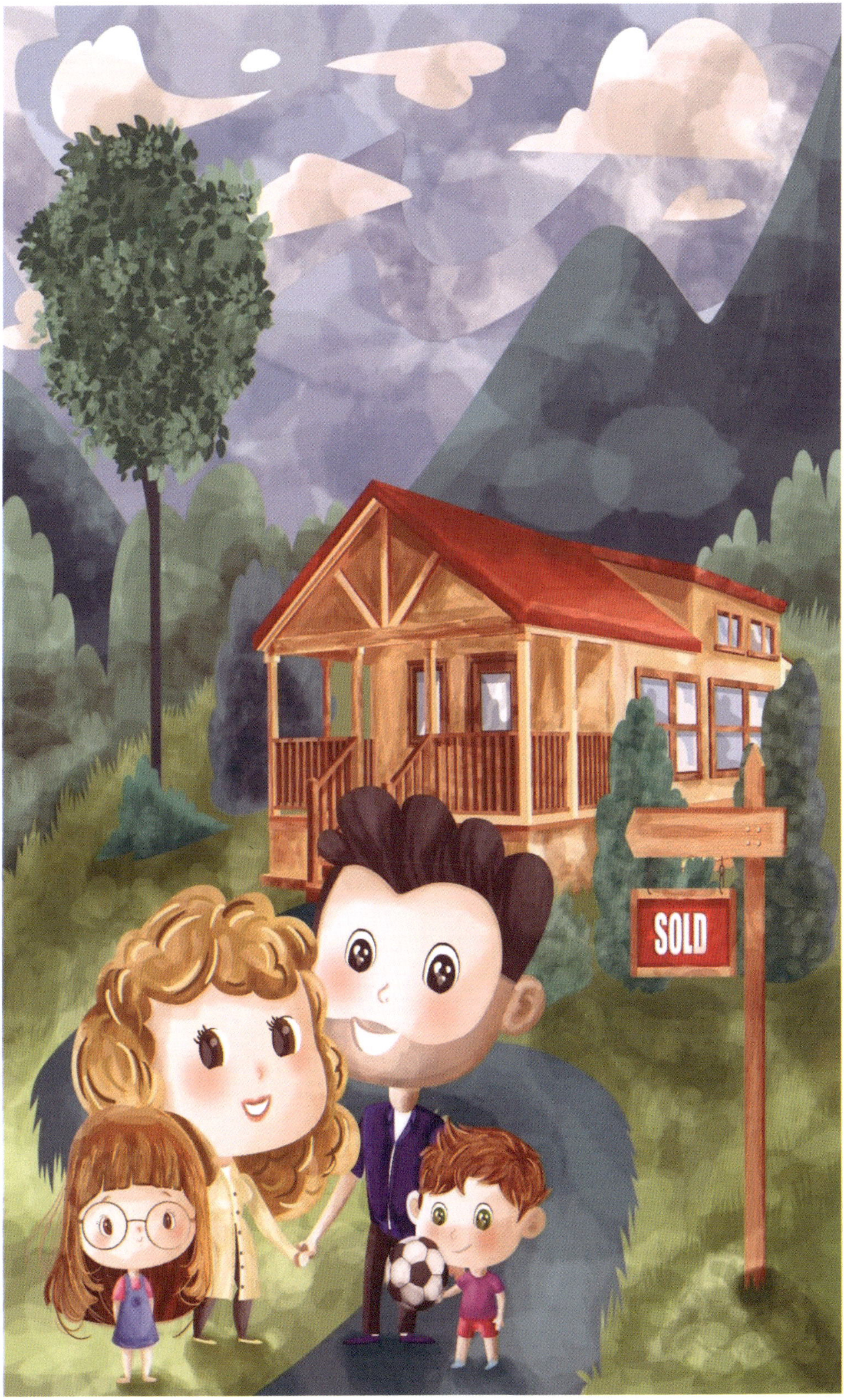
SOLD

Chapter 7

A Different Discovery

I WOKE UP once again. I rubbed my eyes and looked at the time. 7:00. I stretched my arms and yawned.

I opened my closet and went through some clothes. I picked out; tights, denim shorts, an amber t-shirt along with some orange gloves and my black lace-up boots. I did my hair which was two buns and two thick strands of hair hanging off my face on both sides. I put on my glasses and raced downstairs. I was up early, so I made chlieb vo vajci, which is bread, soaked in egg and fried.

I laid the bread slices, each on a plate and put them on the dining table. By the time I was finished, Mum was up. I beamed and got up from my seat.

"First day of school isn't it?" nudged Mum. "Are you excited?"

"Sort of," I stared at the wall. Dad and Jacob woke up. "Morning!" I blubbered.

"Someone's in a good mood," chortled Dad. I told them I was going to get my bag ready and zoomed upstairs into my room. "And remember, your bus is at 8:20 to Masserton Academy!" bawled Mum.

"Alright!" I squawked back. I put my bag over one shoulder as I looked at myself in the mirror and thought,

"I hope I will fit in!"

At exactly 8:20, the bus honked. TOOT! TOOT!

I darted outside and roared, "Bye!"

I shut the door and ran to the bus stop. My stop was three stops away.

I managed to catch the bus on time, sat inside, and focused on steadying my breathing.

I looked at the bus screen. 'NEXT STOP, MASSERTON ACADEMY.'

I picked my bag up and the bus halted to a very heavy stop by a very large and grand looking high school.

I stepped out of the bus and walked toward the main entrance. I sighed and stepped into the majestic building.

As I walked in, I had experienced many strange, new, and mysterious things. I smelt freshly baked buttered croissants and a roast dinner.

I saw glassy, pearl- coloured lockers and a sleek, satiny marble floor, glistening in the cream light. I gasped in awe and thought, *Is this real or a dream?*

I was given a book which had all my information. My locker combination, my classes of the day and so on. I looked through the index and searched for 'Locker Information.'

It seemed my locker was, 'No.99'

I rummaged through all the lockers and eventually found, 99. There was a girl around my age next to it.

She had straight black hair and sapphire-blue eyes. She had a dark blue shirt with her bare belly showing. She turned to me and smiled pleasantly. I smiled back and she said gently, "Hello! I'm Isla."

"I'm Autumn!" I replied eagerly. My first friend of the day, Isla. What a lovely name!

We both grabbed our books, pens, pencils and shut our doors. The bell rang. TRING!

The first class according to the information book was Literacy. I loved writing. I enjoyed it as much as Chemistry.

Isla said she had liked it a lot too. We sat down next to each other. Fortunately, that was put on the seating chart.

As the teacher trudged into the classroom, the entire class stood up and said, "Good morning Miss Leighnour!" in synchrony.

I tried to keep up, but as it was my very first day, I got a bit muddled. "Good morning class!" she spoke, "Now, today we have a new student with us. Say hello to Autumn."

"Good day, Autumn!" the class said rather joyfully. Isla, in sign language, told me to stand up and say, "Good day!"

I sat myself down again. "Well, you have come on a very good day. We were going to recap what we have learnt over the term." She danced and fiddled with her pencil. She talked about correct synonyms, antonyms, and personification. We were given a test paper, but since I had just started, it was just tested on my knowledge.

I got an A+. Miss Leighnour suddenly said, "Those of you who got an A+, stand up."

Autumn's Diary of Dreams

It was just me.

The whole class burst into applause and I was told that I was the new popular girl. I couldn't

believe it. I was going to be popular! The bell rang once again. Me and Isla stomped out of the class.

We went to our lockers but before I could make a fingerprint, every student huddled around me. "What's going on?" I questioned.

"Everyone's coming toward you because you're the new popular girl," she answered.

"AUTUMN MAYSTER, YEAR 7 CLASS 9, PLEASE COME TO THE PRINCIPLE'S OFFICE!" A loud, booming voice came from the speakers.

I gulped with fear and walked to a door which said, 'PRINCIPLE OFFICE'

I knocked politely and waited for an answer. "Come in!" said the gruff voice, "Good day Miss Mayster! I am Principle J. Andre. I have heard you have received an A+ on your exam although you have just joined this school!"

I nodded silently. "Congratulations! You are the new Popular Girl!" He exclaimed noisily. I flinched and said, "Thank you."

A smile formed on the corner of my mouth and walked out of the room. I went back to my locker and went through my book. The next class was ICT. I got my ICT Helper Book, stationary, and slammed the door shut.

Isla came to me. "Do you see that boy over there? He is the Popular Boy. His name is Jake. He is the school's number one jock.

He would come up to one of the girls if he likes them and say something," she explained.

I looked at a twelve year-old boy with hair like Jack Grealish and a Masserton Academy jersey. In an instant, we locked eyes, and he started walking towards me. I felt overwhelmed. Was this going to be like what Isla said? I looked everywhere else but him, and thought, "Oh, what can I do? What can I do?"

Before I could think of anything, he was right in front of me.

Chapter 8

THE CONVERSATION

AS HE STOOD easy, I held my breath until something happened. "Hi. Name's Jake," spoke his friendly voice.

I loosened my muscles and said, "Hi, Jake. My name is Autumn."

"You're the new Popular Girl?" he inquired with a meaningful smile playing on his face.

I nodded. "You're the Popular Boy?" I blurted out.

"Yes!" He laughed.

He seemed quite nice. Mostly gorgeous. The bell suddenly rang. "Alright, I will see you later."

I waved and sighed dreamily. As I walked to ICT, I noticed that Jake was also going there. I sat myself down next to a laptop. He was right behind me. The ICT teacher trudged into the suite. "Good day, class," he spoke in his strong Australian accent, "I am Mr Kings."

His bald head shone in the light. He explained about coding and finding data in many graphics and charts. It was really complicated.

We tried to make a website on our own without assistance. I thought of what could be my website about.

Suddenly, an idea popped into my head. 'What if I could do a web all about Autumn?'

I wrote some good and bad things about Autumn. Hot chocolate and warm, cosy scarves, hats and gloves.

The foul parts were that it is slightly damp and increasingly cold. "That's a good point," said a voice from behind me. It was Jake. "I love Autumn. It's so pretty. Just like you."

I felt blood rush into my cheeks. I continued creating it and felt very proud of myself. By the end of class, I accomplished my mission. The bell gave a big, mighty trill. I pranced out of the ICT suite and went to Isla.

"Hello again!" she bounced.

"Hi!" I grinned.

We walked in the direction of our lockers and there was a letter on mine. The letter wrote, "Dear Autumn, as the new Popular Girl, this is an invitation to the Popular Students Celebration. We hope you consider joining us. The Popular Students. xx."

"What's that?" asked Isla.

"An invitation," I answered.

"Cool! What for?" She bobbed her head up and down.

"This sort of Popular Students Celebration," I folded the paper.

"Nice!" exclaimed Isla.

Autumn's Diary of Dreams

We scanned through our books to find the next class. Chemistry! As I said before, Chemistry is one of my favourite classes. The ringing noise commenced. As we walked toward chemistry class, I saw that there were labels on the back of each chair. These labels had our names. As I searched for my name, I realised that Isla was sitting next to me once again. I gave a sigh of relief.

I also noticed that Jake was on the opposite desk next to ours. I blushed and hid my face. The chemistry teacher smiled. "Good morning, students!" She said in a soft voice, "Today, we are going to record different discoveries we made. These records will be a test as today you have an exam."

I understood what we had to do and got it into my mind. We had to work with the person next to us thankfully.

Me and Isla made all sorts of mixes. We made Dry Ice flames (from my experience), a slimy goo, colourful foam and etcetera. "Wow! You two girls are really eager to explore!" exclaimed the teacher.

Her name was Miss Kapehurst. By the end of class, we had made at least more than twenty different experiments.

Next, we eventually had lunch. I got my tray of food and sat myself besides Isla. The food was so luxurious!

They cooked a selection of roast beef, chicken, or pork. They made cakes, cookies, and chocolates! For a drink, you get asked if you wanted water, juice or flavoured water! Me and Isla chatted about friends and other things.

All of a sudden, an alarm went off. 'BEEP! BOOP! BEEP! BOOP!'

Everyone had a shocked look on their face. "What's going on?!" I roared.

Mr Andre appeared and stated, "System Lockdown!"

WHAT?! I felt so overwhelmed and frightened that I fainted.

Light. Sound. I was awakening.

I saw multiple people surrounding me. "Auts?" an echoing sound quivered. I gasped and sat up. "What happened?" My tone trembled.

I had a sudden flashback. "An alarm."

A deep silence hung in the air. Isla, Jake, Mr Andre, and the dinner ladies all gathered around me.

A cold prickling feeling smacked my back. Isla helped me up, but no matter what, I felt weak. Mr Andre said I needed some rest. After a while, I was strong enough to stand and walk. I looked out of a window and spotted something.

A large, black clump of mist. My eyes widened and I turned swiftly to Mr Andre. "Am I hallucinating?" I laughed with a hysterical feeling. He shook his head, unfortunately. I had another flashback. "The dream, "I whispered.

"What dream?" Isla tilted her head.

"A dream I had ever since I was a little girl. An enormous cloud of jet black mist."

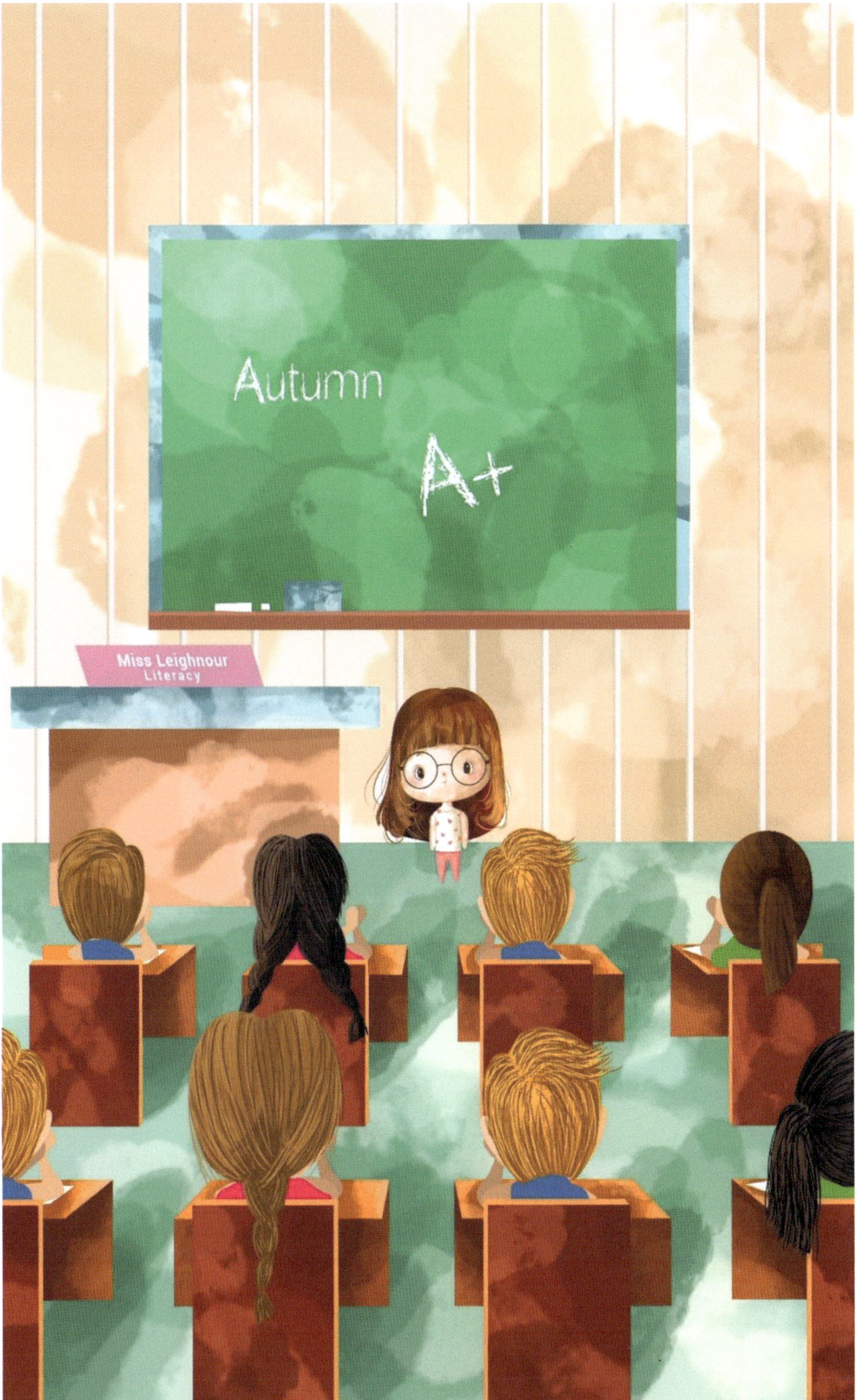
Autumn
A+
Miss Leighnour
Literacy

Chapter 9

JINX

THE INKY, black fog turned slowly and faced us. It's red, glowing eyes stared at me and his toothy, menacing grin shone into my eyes. He spoke in his deep, cracking voice. "I am Jinx and I declare that I will take over this very dimension!" He levitated with six arms flowing in unison to his body. My heart raced swiftly with fear.

I thought about Mum, Dad, Jacob and Ascher. I felt tears building up. I put my hand in my pocket and felt something. It was the picture of Mum and Dad holding me. I sniffled and said courageously, "Right! We need to stop that horrifying chunk of darkness."

Everyone looked at one another and shrugged. I sighed. "How?" asked Isla.

"We make a plan."

I fell onto a sofa. Mr Andre came back with a cup of tea for everyone. As he handed a mug to me, I stared out of the window, occupied with wondrous thoughts. Jinx spoke once again, "I shall have now jinxed everyone in this worthless place. Once I finished this silly little city, I will take over the world, eat the Solar System, steal the Universe and break the ominiverse!"

He raised his voice with a loud, sinister cackle, "Pain and fear shall only make me bigger so get frightened and I can do thrilling things!"

"Wait," I narrowed my eyes. "If he had jinxed the entire city, we would know how we were jinxed."

"Then let's find out!" Jake ran ahead of us.

"You go. We'll stay here," whimpered one of the dinner ladies.

I smiled and said, "Just keep safe. Also, don't let your jinx get to you."

Both the ladies nodded. I ran back to find out. We walked into the main corridor by the lockers.

"What if it is our favourite class and we can't get inside?" suggested Jake.

We walked towards our favourite classes. "STOP!" I howled. "We need to be careful we don't get locked in."

It wasn't that.

"Maybe it is one of our favourite hobbies," Isla spun.

We went to do our hobbies. I went to write a poem in Literacy Class and as I lay my pencil tip on the paper, the pencil flipped out of my hand. I tried again. Flip, flip, flip, flip, flip, went the pencil.

"I know my jinx." I sighed disappointedly, "At least my jinx isn't that I can't read books."

Jake was in the gymnasium about to kick a football. As he was going to kick it, a large invisible shield repelled Jake away. He tried once more. BANG!

I went to see Isla. She was going to pick up a ball but it was swept away from her with a loud swoosh.

She tried once again. Eventually, her energy drained out and she gave up.

Mr Andre was going to write a letter to his boss but all the words were invisible. One more time. Nothing.

"Well, at least we know that we can't do those things." I exhaled.

"What do we do now?" asked Isla and turned to Mr Andre.

He shrugged his shoulders. Everyone looked at me hopefully. I pointed at myself questionably and groaned.

"We need to create a plot." I say confidently.

I instructed Isla to find four pencils, Jake to find some rulers and Mr Andre to find some paper in his office. We made a blue print styled plan with annotations. We were ready.

Chapter 10

THE PLAN

ME, ISLA, JAKE and Mr Andre started making the plan. In no time, we created a plan like no other.

When it was ready, we went to prepare ourselves. We all agreed to find a 'weapon' to protect and defend.

Jake went to find a basketball hoop since he was strong enough. Isla was going to find a baseball bat because it was the only thing to do with balls that she could hold. Mr Andre found one of his belts. I, last of all, had found a large pole. Perfect! Weapons. Check! Now for armour, Jake went to find his jock uniform and a rugby helmet. Isla went to find some of the school knights armour. I said it wasn't worth it because if we were going to be, we would be injured anyway.

I found the school kitchens knife sharpeners, so I sharpened my pole. It was more like an axe then. Isla took off all the armour other than the helmet. Mr Andre just put on layers and layers and layers and layers and layers and layers of clothes, since he hadn't any armour. Armour. Check!

"I feel like we are missing something." I tapped my toe impatiently.

"Oh yes, I know what we're missing," I jumped, "To pray and hope for eternal victory."

I prayed so that we would have victory and destroy the horrifying beast. I looked out of the window once again.

He was growing, and fast! "We best get to it," stamped Jake, "Or he'll get too big for us."

We all nodded in unison. We walked out of the building cautiously in case of any traps.

I bobbed my head. We went behind his slimy, fat tentacles. "We must watch each other's backs." I whispered.

"On three. One, two... three!"

I chopped five gooey legs but they grew back. "No reaction." Isla tilted her head.

"I see," I said with my normal voice, "this is his deaf and blind spot so he can't see or hear us."

Everyone said, "Ohhh!"

I tried to execute another set of legs, but this time, all of them.

"SLISH, SLOSH, PLOP!" went the legs.

The chopped legs on the ground just withered away into the breeze and the parts remaining on it's body squelched and grew into a new bunch. I gave a "Seriously" look on my face.

We then went inside to think of another plan. But this time, better! We made another blue print styled plan to keep us organised. It was harder to make than the previous one as it had more clear annotations but what brought me relief was the fact that it was neatly made.

The plan was ready, once again.

The plan was, let's just say, more intricate and complex. It was simple and unique. We trudged outside into danger. Again, we creeped up behind him. As we did that, I imagined a crescendo increasing in pitch.

It felt so realistic that I winced to the pitch of the peak. I signalled Isla to take the left side and Jake to take the right. Mr Andre was back up with more Plan B weapons. I counted down from three.

Once I got to one, I slid on the now dead grass under Jinx and threw my axe upwards. 'SLICE!'

A big cut was made by his legs that oozed a purple goo. I backwards rolled myself up and dodged the substance.

"Blood." I scoffed. "What now? What can we do?" Mr Andre uttered.

I tapped my chin in thought. My eyes narrowed again. "I don't know…" I admitted.

"Let's get into the school. It's getting dark." Jake went towards the main entrance.

We went to the gym and had a shower. Suddenly, a clattering sound echoed through the corridor. "What was that?!" we all whispered.

We grabbed hold of our weapons and slowly stepped closer to the sound. It got louder and louder until a yelling sound started. I stepped forwards gripping my axe taking up momentum. The sound came right in front of me. I held my breath. *This is it.* I thought. Three, two, one.

Wait. It turned out the sound wasn't a disgusting, horrifying creature going to ambush us, it was Miss Kapehurst, the chemistry teacher. "Oh! I am so sorry!" she apologized, "I thought you guys were a bunch of disgusting, horrifying creatures."

We explained what had happened and who is left in the building. "Well, I do say! I could even help you, you know, with all the weaponry and things. Maybe I could help as in first aid." she suggested.

An hour later, it was terribly dark. That was a very bad thing because, Jinx is black and darkness is black.

It was very hard to spot him. We settled ourselves into the teacher's lounge. I read some of the school's Moby Dick. I read four chapters but couldn't go to sleep. I sighed and thought of Mum, Dad, Jacob and Ascher. I sniffled and a salty tear glided down my face. "You okay?" whispered a voice in the darkness.

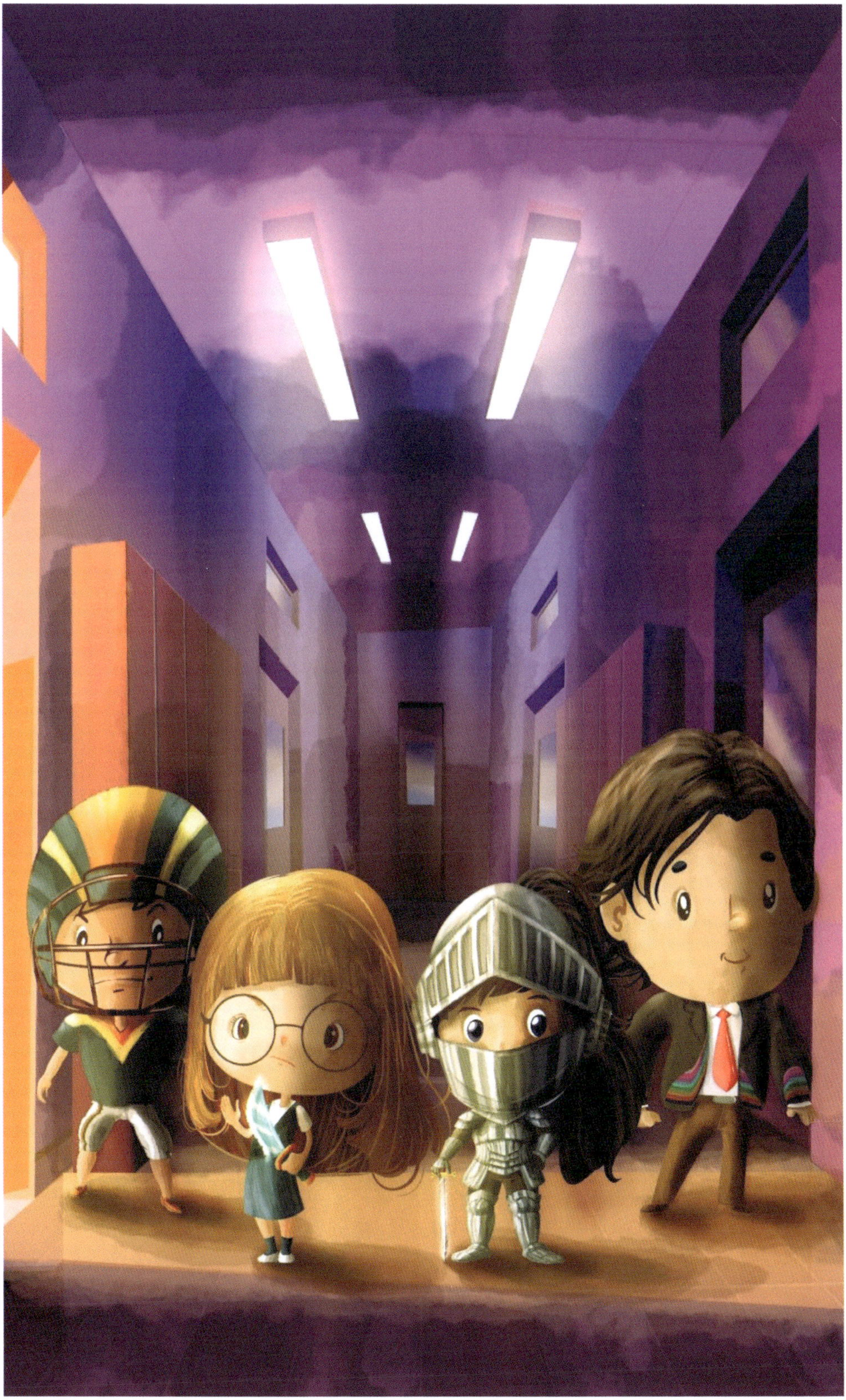

Chapter 11

BRAVERY AND FEAR

THE VOICE was Isla. "Yes." I answered, my voice cracking.

My eyes felt heavy, my hands were weak until, I fell into a deep slumber. Twitch. I had a dream.

Jinx was kidnapping my beloved family, wrapping his tentacles onto them. I awoke with a shock. It was sunrise.

I checked the time. It was 6:20. I read some more Moby Dick until everyone rose from their rest.

First, Isla was up. Then Jake woke up, Mr Andre woke up and finally, Miss Kapehurst.

We all went down to have some food. We went to the kitchen. As Mr Andre opened the pantry doors, there were many sorts of food. Frozen, baked and so on! Our food was like as if it was served in one of those fancy French restaurants. We had bread and butter, fresh croissants with a blackberry and raspberry jam, fatty bacon, saucy beans, potato hash browns, mini cocktail sausages and a Swiss chocolate selection.

Autumn's Diary of Dreams

I ate. Ohh. All of those scrumptious flavours created a tasty explosion of deliciousness that made my mouth water constantly. "Well that was lovely." squeaked Miss Kapehurst. Everyone nodded in agreement.

"Those croissants were impeccable!" I scoffed eloquently.

"The absolute best." sighed Isla.

"Magnifique!!!" exclaimed Mr. Andre.

"That was bussin'…" mumbled Jake, licking his fingers with pleasure. Nobody didn't like it. It was perfect.

Once everybody had finished their glorious breakfast, we went upstairs and found some clothes in Lost Property. I found a beige crop top, black, leather bike gloves, a denim skirt, and some red lace-up boots.

We were almost ready for the tough day ahead. We also went to put our recent clothes in the laundry room.

Yes. This school had almost everything! We headed back to the teacher's lounge again to get our weapons.

I had only then realised that Miss Kapehurst's weapon was a belt set with knives, large and small. I smiled and bounced my head. "Let's go to Mr. Andre's office to make another plan," suggested Jake.

"Please, call me Jackson." he insisted.

"Okay, Jackson." smirked Isla.

We strolled to Jackson's office and got some stationary. We planned. It took at least an hour to finish it, it took five minds, it took a few disagreements but it was all worth it. No suggestions too big, no idea too small. It took us only three or four attempts to get ready. Again. The plan was unique, the plan was great, the plan was unstoppable.

We sneaked outside and creeped up behind Jinx. I pointed Isla to go underneath.

Jackson went to take one side and Jake the other. Miss Kapehurst stayed behind and I climbed up on him.

I put up five fingers, four, three, two, one! "STAB!" Everybody went through the very centre. I jumped off. The creature was down. Slowly, his body disintegrated into thin air. "YES!" everyone cheered.

"We did it. We actually did it." I spoke quietly.

The sky brightened, the flowers bloomed, and people reappeared. Mum, Dad, Jacob, and Ascher appeared.

"Mum! Dad! Jacob!" I ran to them. I gave them a big, tight hug. I sobbed with relief. My cheeks hot with tears and my belly warm with joy. "Come on my rose, let's go home." said a soft voice. Mum.

Chapter 12

THE MEMORY

I WOKE UP at 7:00a.m. I hopped out of bed and took in all my things. Home. I was finally home. I changed into a beige crop top, black, leather bike gloves and red lace up boots.

I brushed my hair and curled it. I put my glasses on and jumped downstairs. "No jumping off the stairs!" shouted Mum. "Oops! Sorry. Got a bit used to jumping off…"

"Don't say the name!" screamed another voice. The voice turned out to be Jacob. I looked at him. He seemed so scared. "I get it Jacob, it's traumatizing." I gave him a cuddle. A smile grew on his face. "Can we still go see the football match tomorrow?" he pleaded.

"Well, since me and your Mum found out that we have enough money, we can." Dad came from upstairs.

'RING! RING!' My phone was vibrating on the table. As I went to pick it up, a message popped up. I read it and gasped. "What?!" Jacob shrieked.

"Oh my--" I hesitated, "we have been invited to a special meeting with THE Prime Minister!"

"WELL WE BETTER GET FANCY!!" he yodelled.

"Wait! There's more..." I read and read, "since me, Isla, Jake, Jackson and Miss Kapehurst technically saved the world, we are all rewarded with £10,000!!!"

Everyone looked at each other in astonishment. "When is the meeting?" asked Mum.

"Today, 19:20." I said calmly.

I then went to the cabinet and got some eggs, butter and chives and made simple scrambled eggs.

Once I had finished, I went to prepare my bag. My bus was out. "See you soon Autumn!" chuckled Dad. I hopped into the bus and everyone on the bus was gathering around me. "You're one of the kids that saved the entire omniverse?" they questioned. But before I could finish nodding, a flicker of amazement and awe rushed through the crowd. *Well, I am officially famous!* I thought with a giggle.

I arrived at school. As I stepped inside, I came in to witness another audience. "Okay, what's going on?" I asked. "You were one of the people who got famous for literally saving not only the universe but the omniverse!" said a distant voice. I walked to my locker and met Isla.

"Apparently, we're famous." Isla raised her eyebrow and clasped her hands together in excitement. I looked around and saw an enormous, marble statue of me, Isla, Jake, Jackson and Miss Kapehurst battling Jinx. I examined the inspiring monument and thought, 'I really did save the world...'

Me and Isla slammed the doors and strolled up the corridor. We bumped into someone. "Jackso—Mr. Andre, hello." I hesitated. He smiled politely as his phone begun to ring. He picked it up and chatted away.

RING! The bell trilled. We had French class. Uh-oh! I thought. Hopefully, the teacher wasn't

going to be like Mrs Jeanues. I crossed my fingers as tight as possible and stepped into the classroom.

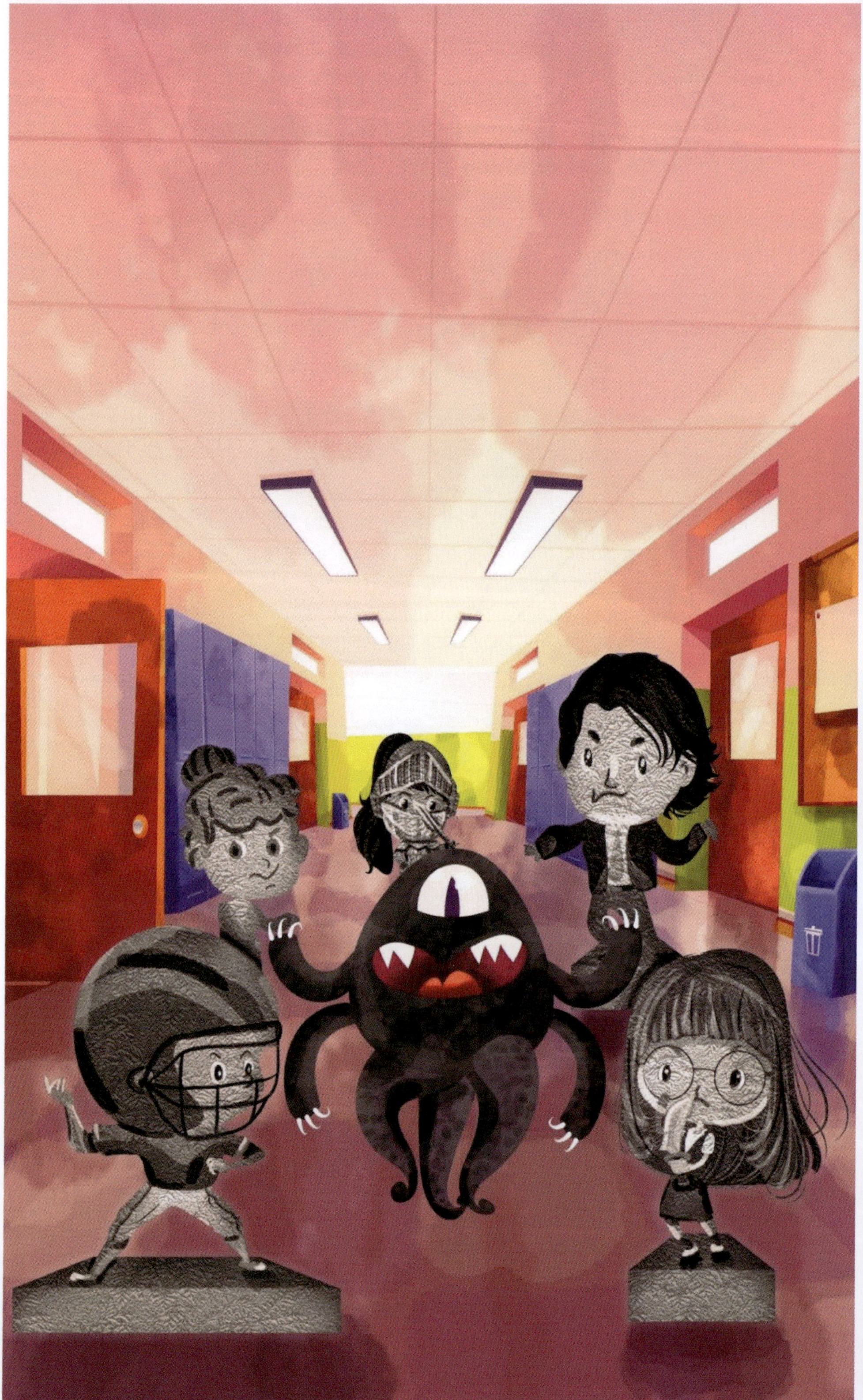

Chapter 13
Miss Clémentine

I HOPED, AS I got into the classroom, that the teacher would be as spectacular as all the others. I pointed my toes onto the snowy-white and ash-grey floor and had felt many things. I felt love, hate, fear and trust. These emotions made me a bit all over the place. I sat myself down and waited for the teacher.

"Oh, oh sorry Monsieur André!" said an increasing voice.

"Bonjour les enfants!" sang a sweet voice, "I am Mademoiselle Clémentine!"

Each and every part of anxiousness and fear inside me fluttered away. We learnt about language structures in this class. For our starter, we did simple sentences, for example, "Jake jouait au football sur le terrain. Il a marqué plusieurs fois et a remporté le match." I got a F+.

It was hard to say and spell it but once you do it repeatedly, you get it. At 10:00, we had a bit of mathematics. We had to say the longer term because we were too old to say 'maths'.

It was so hard! The teacher Mr Smith said it was simple mathematics/arithmetic. I hadn't known at least half the questions. I didn't know that it was actually an exam until the papers were given out.

D-! The last time I got a D- was when I joined in Milton Keynes. I was so disappointed. "How was French class?" asked Isla.

"Terrible!" I shouted in a French accent.

"How about mathematics?" she inquired.

"Simply unacceptable!" I groaned. I flopped towards the lockers and got my instructions book.

The next class was Literacy. Miss Leighnour wasn't in the class. Instead, there was a tall man with glasses and hazelnut hair. He wore a business suit looking blazer and trousers. "A very good morning, class." he stood, "I am Mr Matterns. Miss Leighnour is not here since she is unwell so I shall teach you Literacy."

We did an exam. I finally realised that we have an entire school day of exams and test. I put my name at the top box. There was a text underneath so I read it. I had to answer questions about the text. The short story was a fable. The fable was, 'The Fox and the Grapes.'

The first question said, "What is the moral of this story?"

I wrote in my neatest handwriting, "Some people will disparage what they cannot achieve or have for themselves."

When I got my paper back, I looked for the score. A+! I had done it! Hallelujah! I did a little dance in my seat.

Chapter 14
A Great Experience

IT WAS EVENTUALLY lunch time. It was another lavish feast. Me and Isla chatted about. I kept looking at the clock ready for the time when Jinx had striked. Three, two, one. Nothing happened. I sighed in relief.

I gladly ate and talked. 13:30, the bell yelled. The next class was P.E. I hadn't had this class in this school yet. Our coach was Coach Franks. I went into the gymnasium and hoped that the sports would be easier than the previous school. Thankfully, for the warm up, we did some simple exercises only.

The main lesson was gymnastics, one of my favourites! We learnt to do cartwheels and handstand flatbacks. We even learnt to do walkovers. I had already known all of this so I zoomed through it all.

We did that for a shocking two hours! 16:00, at last, we could go home. My bus was out and early so I couldn't delay. I fell back into a seat rested my eyes. 'TOOT! TOOT!'

The bus honked at me for I was asleep. I ran inside and leaned on the door exhaustedly. *Friday was finally here.* I thought.

"FRIDAY!" yodelled a voice. It was Jacob. "TOMORROW, WE'RE GONNA SEE THE BIG

MATCH!"

I heard a giggle coming from the kitchen. I walked in. "Ah! Shoes off!" Mum stopped without looking at me.

I kicked my boots off and trudged upstairs. I sighed and laid in my bed dreaming myself to a deep sleep.

I dreamt of books as usual. BANG!

A sound woke me up. "JACOB JAMES MAYSTER! WHAT HAVE YOU DONE?!!?" shrieked Mum.

I raced down to see what had happened. I gasped. The kitchen window had been smashed. "You are grounded for a month!" she yelled.

Chapter 15

THE FORGIVENESS

JACOB WENT OUTSIDE in dismay. I followed him. He sat out on the patio with his grazed knees to his chest.

"Don't bother cheering me up." He sobbed. I gave him a big hug and helped him delete his sadness.

"We'll make it up to Mum." I whispered. As I embraced him, I felt his sadness and guilt. I called a window fixer person while Mum was out shopping. He fixed it in ten minutes. I thanked him and said my farewells. I wished that Mum would forgive Jacob and everything would be okay.

Mum came home with bags in each hand. I listened through the walls. "WHAT?!" Mum gasped with shock.

"Kids!" she squawked. We walked in slow-motion towards her. "Thank you, dear children! Because of what you have done, I forgive you!"

Me and Jacob gave Mum a big squeeze. Dad came home that very second. "James! They've fixed it!" "Well, I never!" he placed his hat and hung his coat.

"Actually, I paid for a window fixer to have it fixed." I admitted truthfully.

"Oh! That was a very ambitious thing to do." Mum tucked my hair behind my ears.

I felt proud of myself. I decided to get changed into my woollen dress and tights. I felt warm and cosy.

I placed my heated hand on my heart and felt it beat. BOOM! BOOM! BOOM

I had a sudden flashback. I felt pain, love, passion, and hate. I closed my eyes to the sensation and smiled. I sat in the lounge and curled up on the corner sofa. I rested my eyelids and experienced the

emotional mix. I smiled and frowned at the same time, awaiting my future……

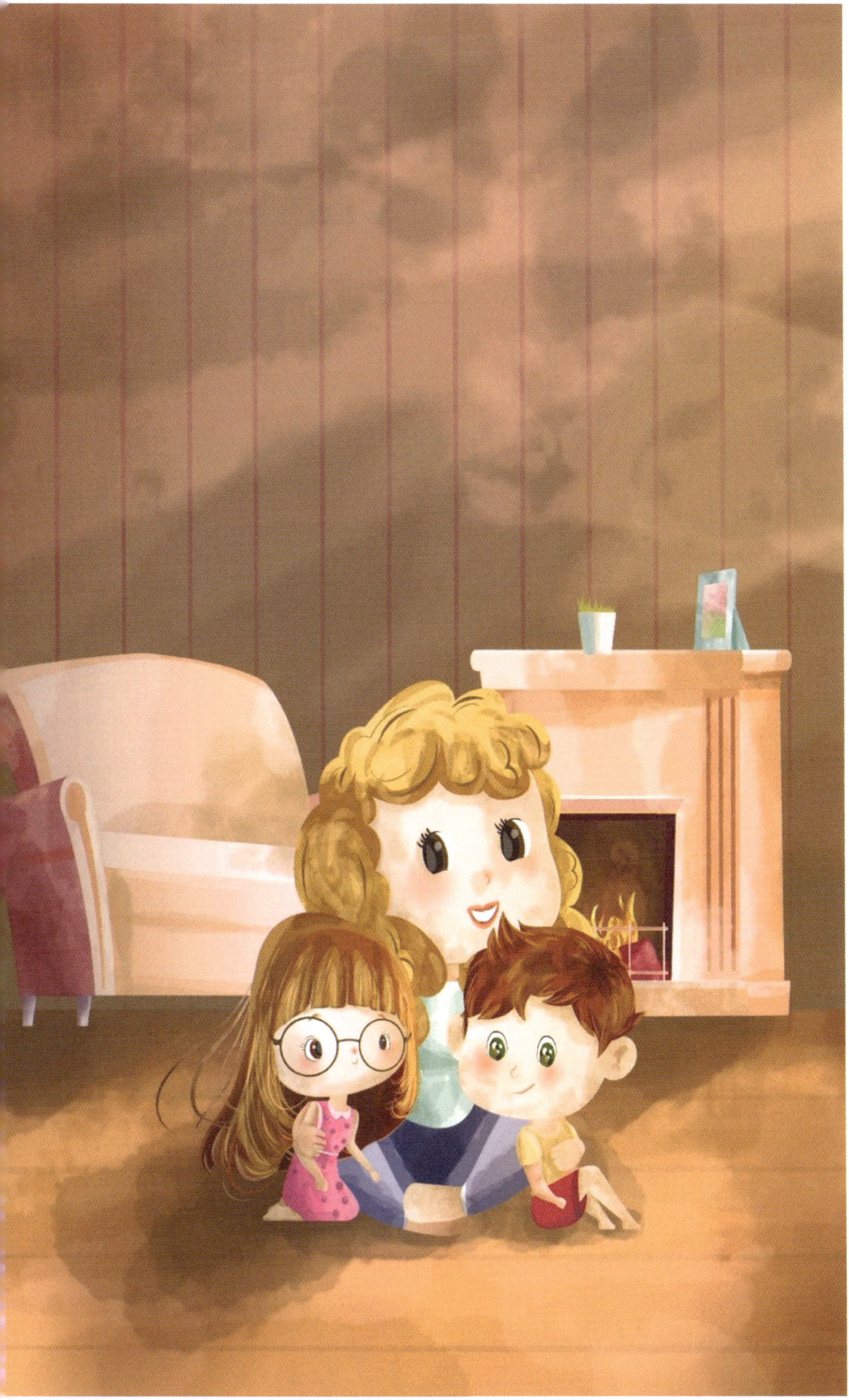

EPILOGUE

This is now the finale of Autumn Mayster's stories. Or is it? They all enjoyed their new life in Manchester and had lived the best of it. Jacob got what he dreamt of, the football match and an experience of a lifetime. Manchester seems like it's their last destination. Autumn had realised that it could have been their final and forever home. Mum and Dad had eventually found a perfect job to provide a living they've always wanted, with security and stability in their lives. Autumn was awed in her environment and had lived her life openly with many opportunities to fulfil her dreams where she could grow her roots.

This is not the end of Autumn's journeys…she will come back soon with more adventures. She will be ready for YOU. Yes, you. Will she consider coming again? That is for you to decide……

Printed in Great Britain
by Amazon